To make Asleep

Laura

2017

EVERYDAY
EVANGELISM

Practical Tips to Use Today

Show Them We Are
Christians by Our Love

Laura Yang

WESTBOW
P R E S S®
A DIVISION OF THOMAS NELSON
& ZONDERVAN

All Scripture quotations, unless otherwise indicated, are taken from THE HOLY BIBLE, NEW INTERNATIONAL VERSION®, NIV® Copyright © 1973, 1978, 1984, 2011 by Biblica, Inc.® Used by permission. All rights reserved worldwide.

WestBow Press books may be ordered through booksellers or by contacting:

WestBow Press
A Division of Thomas Nelson & Zondervan
1663 Liberty Drive
Bloomington, IN 47403
www.westbowpress.com
1 (866) 928-1240

Because of the dynamic nature of the Internet, any web addresses or links contained in this book may have changed since publication and may no longer be valid. The views expressed in this work are solely those of the author and do not necessarily reflect the views of the publisher, and the publisher hereby disclaims any responsibility for them.

Any people depicted in stock imagery provided by Thinkstock are models, and such images are being used for illustrative purposes only. Certain stock imagery © Thinkstock.

ISBN: 978-1-5127-2227-7 (sc)
ISBN: 978-1-5127-2226-0 (e)

Library of Congress Control Number: 2015919904

Print information available on the last page.

WestBow Press rev. date: 02/04/2016

Acknowledgements

To My Father in Heaven—Hallowed be Thy Name! Thank you for saving a sinner like me. My Savior Jesus Christ, no words can acknowledge your unfathomable sacrifice. Thank you for indwelling me with your Holy Spirit. To the Apostle Paul, your life is a testament that God can save anyone! Oh that I could live like you: "sold out" for God.

To my husband George, I love you. Bryce and Tristan, I am blessed that God chose me to be your mother. Mom and Dad, thank you for raising me in a Christian home and for being my biggest cheerleaders. To my dear friend Jana Cain, I am eternally grateful for the part you played in leading me to Christ and for your ongoing wisdom.

Laura McCorvey and Jana Cain: I cherish our friendship. Thank you for believing that it was God's will for me to write *Everyday Evangelism*. Without your ongoing support and prayers this project may never have come to fruition. To Bart McCorvey and Kevin Smith—your encouragement gave me the confidence to go for it!

To Linh Ding, Mary Kono, and Laura Drabkin, our "Monday Morning Bible Studies" and your words of affirmation are forever etched on my heart and in my soul. Lisa Hinton, your contributions have been priceless. Lisset Becker, God will use the amazing graphic arts skills that He has given you to save more souls through *Everyday Evangelism*. And Westbow Press, I appreciate all of your assistance.

Lastly, I am eternally grateful to my church family: Pacific Coast Church. I will never forget how you took care of me and my family during crisis. Pastor Mark and Susan Ambrose, Pastor Dan and Betty Anderson: each of you demonstrates you are Christians by your love.

Contents

Introduction

Do you struggle with sharing your Christian faith? You are not alone! Most Christians do. In fact, only two percent of church members invite an unchurched person to church. Ninety-eight percent of churchgoers never extend an invitation in a given year.[1]

Satan uses fear to stop Christians from sharing our faith: it's one of his strategies to prevent the spread of the gospel. And it's working. While God is sovereign, the Christian population in America is shrinking rapidly.[2]

The Enemy delights when we pass up opportunities to share Christ. First of all, our failure to act prevents the possible salvation of another. Secondly, we wallow in guilt and begin to lose confidence. Yet God has so much more for us! When we step outside of our comfort zones to share the gospel, the "good news" of Jesus Christ, God infuses us with indescribable joy. This exhilarating joy will propel us to continue sharing our faith.

Let's begin to grasp the magnitude of what God can, and wants to, accomplish through us. He has equipped us with his Holy Spirit—the same power that raised Jesus from the dead. God has given Christians the amazing privilege of sharing His life and death message.

Christians like to be comfortable—just like everyone else. We spend the majority of our time furthering our own faith. We go to church, attend Bible Study, and enjoy the fellowship of other believers. While these activities are crucial, as Christians our priority is to invest in the salvation of others.

> *"Therefore go and make disciples of all nations, baptizing them in the name of the Father and of the Son and of the Holy Spirit, and teaching them to obey everything I have commanded you. And surely I am with you always, to the very end of the age" (Matthew 28:19-20).*

These verses are known as "The Great Commission." They are Jesus' final instructions to all believers. The Great Commission is Jesus' top priority for us. That is why it is the topic of the first tip in this book. "Go" is an action word! If ever there were a time in history for Christians to act immediately, it is now.

In the course of writing *Everyday Evangelism*, God made it evident that this book should highlight three foundational principles. These principles are not rocket science—they are straight from Scripture. However, we all need reminders from time to time.

The first principle is that evangelism, or sharing the good news of Jesus Christ, is something God wants us to do every day. He wants our lives to be "others-focused"—not simply when it is convenient. Secondly, we have no reason to fear sharing the gospel. God has equipped us with his Holy Spirit—he will even give us the words at exactly the right time.

The third principle is that evangelism is only to be done in love. Think of the people God used to influence your conversion to Christianity. Did they love you? Listen to you? Care for you? Did they kindly tell you about Jesus, possibly taking the time to invite and bring you to an event? Or did they criticize, judge, argue, and debate? The Bible does not command Christians to tell others of their sin. The Bible instructs us only to sing the praises of Jesus and to share what he has done for us.

The practical tips in this book are intended to help spur you to action—today! It is my humble hope that God will use *Everyday Evangelism* as a tool to foster your growth in lifestyle evangelism. Sharing the gospel is our purpose as Christians, and when we are living our purpose, God rewards us—with unparalleled joy. God will abundantly multiply the harvest through your obedience and intentionality to share the good news of Jesus Christ.

Use of *Everyday Evangelism*

1. Be intentional. Ask God to reveal opportunities to use these tips. He will—and don't second guess. Seize the opportunity!

2. Use one of these suggestions immediately. Highlight tips that appeal to you and implement them at your own pace. There is no sequence, nor rule, that you must use them all.

3. These tips are NOT a checklist. Use them to build relationships, serve others in word and deed, and utilize the Holy Spirit within you to share the gospel.

4. Enlist an accountability partner. This is a huge benefit because each of you can share the amazing joy you will experience when God uses you to plant, water, or harvest a seed.

5. Place *Everyday Evangelism* in a visible location. When you notice you are becoming a little too self-focused and "comfortable," re-read these tips to motivate you to "go make disciples."

Biblical Reassurance Tips

#1 Follow the Instructions
#2 Grasp the Magnitude and Go For It!
#3 Accept the Job Promotion
#4 Stop Second-Guessing Yourself
#5 Tell Others What God Has Done for You
#6 Learn to Accept Opposition

Biblical Reassurance Tip #1
FOLLOW THE INSTRUCTIONS

When all else fails, read the instructions.

> *"Therefore go and make disciples of all nations, baptizing them in the name of the Father and of the Son and of the Holy Spirit, and teaching them to obey everything I have commanded you. And surely I am with you always, to the very end of the age" (Matthew 28:19-20).*

These verses are Jesus' final instructions to all believers. Known as the "Great Commission," Jesus commands Christians to "go make disciples." As we go out into the world, leading our everyday lives, we are to tell others about Jesus.

We do not need to be afraid to share our faith—to evangelize. Evangelism simply means to share the gospel. And the gospel is the "good news" of Jesus Christ! Consider the consequences had someone not shared this good news with you.

Evangelism is not an activity for Christians to check off a list. It is not something reserved only for missionaries, pastors, or Billy Graham. It should simply be part of the everyday Christian lifestyle.

Jesus expects us to finish His work where he left off. He knew it wouldn't be easy—we are up against Satan. That is one reason why Jesus indwells us with his Holy Spirit—so we won't have to go it alone. The Great Commission reminds us that He will always be with us.

Has God ever instructed you to do something that is not in your own best interest? No! That is because intentionality to fulfill the Great Commission will also bring you exhilarating joy.

Biblical Reassurance Tip #2
GRASP THE MAGNITUDE AND GO FOR IT!

Even before you were born, God had a plan for you. You are made in His image and He has given you talents to accomplish amazing things for His purpose.

> *"For we are God's handiwork, created in Christ Jesus to do good works,*
> *which God prepared in advance for us to do" (Ephesians 2:10).*

If you are saved, you are qualified to tell others about Jesus. God has empowered you with his Holy Spirit—the same power that raised Jesus from the dead! You do not have to be a theological expert. Start applying what you know today!

> *"The Spirit you received does not make you slaves, so that*
> *you live in fear again; rather, the Spirit you received brought*
> *about your adoption to sonship" (Romans 8:15).*

Begin to grasp the magnitude of what God wants to accomplish through you. He wants to work through you to prevent your family, friends, and even strangers from the repercussions of eternal separation from God! While the job can be challenging, it yields amazing rewards on earth and for eternity.

Biblical Reassurance Tip #3
ACCEPT THE JOB PROMOTION

When Jesus ascended to Heaven, this created a huge job vacancy on Earth—"to go and make disciples."

We are Christ's ambassadors. Ambassadors represent their homeland while living in a foreign country. Christians represent Heaven while living in a world that is not our home. Each of us is God's spokesperson while living on Earth.

> *"We are therefore Christ's ambassadors, as though God were making his appeal through us. We implore you on Christ's behalf: Be reconciled to God" (2 Corinthians 5:20).*

Have you ever felt underpaid and underappreciated? You will never feel that way if you prioritize your role as Christ's ambassador! Have you ever been jealous of people who have made it to the "top"? Perhaps they are CEO's or owners of successful businesses? While they make crucial decisions for a lifetime, Christ's ambassadors can affect life on earth and for all eternity!

In some respects, it can seem like the Christian life is characterized by delayed gratification. However, all of God's commands are for our best interest. There is no price tag high enough for the exhilarating joy you will feel when you live out the Great Commission.

Biblical Reassurance Tip #4
STOP SECOND-GUESSING YOURSELF

When you share God's Word, you may never see evidence that you made an impact. However, you can be sure that the Holy Spirit, working through you, will continue to permeate your listener's heart. Do not anguish over thoughts like, "if only I had said this or that!" Self-doubt is from Satan, attempting to preoccupy you from sharing the gospel.

> *"...so is my word that goes out from my mouth: it will not return to me empty, but will accomplish what I desire and achieve the purpose for which I sent it" (Isaiah 55:11).*

This verse reassures us that God's Word does not return void. Trust God that His Word, spoken through you, will continue to be used just as He intended.

Do not become discouraged if you aren't successful in leading someone to salvation. God desires that no one perish, so He is constantly placing experiences and people in the path of others to prepare their hearts. Wouldn't you like for God to use you?

"So neither the one who plants nor the one who waters is anything, but only God, who makes things grow. The one who plants and the one who waters have one purpose, and they will each be rewarded according to their own labor. For we are co-workers in God's service..." (1 Corinthians 3:7-9).

5

Biblical Reassurance Tip #5
TELL OTHERS WHAT GOD HAS DONE FOR YOU

Do not wait for others to ask about your faith! God is constantly opening doors for you. Pray that God will make you aware of these opportunities. Equip yourselves to be ready to share the gospel message and a brief personal testimony at any time (See Critical Conversation Tips #1 and #2).

"But in your hearts revere Christ as Lord. Always be prepared to give an answer to everyone who asks you to give the reason for the hope that you have. But do this with gentleness and respect" (Peter 3:15).

When you share your faith, use Jesus as your model. Did Jesus have a "hell, fire, and brimstone" approach? No. He spoke the truth in love. Guard yourself from being arrogant, self-righteous, and condescending. Do not debate, and if someone indicates they don't want to talk about Jesus, by all means oblige. If it is appropriate, perhaps close the discussion by saying, "I'm sorry, I didn't mean to offend you. I just get so excited about the difference Jesus has made in my life."

Do not let those who oppose your beliefs prevent you from continuing to share the good news. There are plenty of people who are ready to hear the gospel message. Matthew 9:37 reminds us that "the harvest is plentiful."

"Give praise to the LORD, proclaim his name; make known among the nations what he has done. Sing to him, sing praise to him; tell of all his wonderful acts" (Psalm 105:1-2).

Psalm 105:1-2 highlights that evangelism is really quite basic (and non-threatening). Proclaim the name of Jesus! Tell everyone the wonderful things he has done for you. And tell others he can do the same for them!

Biblical Reassurance Tip #6
LEARN TO ACCEPT OPPOSITION

As you share your faith, some people will be receptive and others will be offended. As evangelism becomes your daily lifestyle, you will begin to accept opposition and ridicule.

As an example, my mother has been dubbed "the Soup Lady" by a not-so-friendly neighbor. She knows my mother is a Christian and that she brings homemade soup to anyone in need. When this same lady fell ill, my mom brought her soup, too. The neighbor was incredibly appreciative, and now she is pleasant and has dropped the nickname. Through the power of the Holy Spirit, my mother loved her "enemy," causing her cynical neighbor's heart to be softened.

"If you love those who love you, what credit is that to you? Even sinners love those who love them. And if you do good to those who are good to you, what credit is that to you? Even sinners do that... But love your enemies, do good to them, and lend to them without expecting to get anything back. Then your reward will be great, and you will be children of the Most High..."
(Luke 6:32-35)

When you are scoffed at and made fun of, this persecution is evidence that you are sharing in Christ's sufferings. You will grow to have compassion for these naysayers, as did Jesus on the cross, when he cried, "Father forgive them for they do not know what they are doing" (Luke 23:34).

"That is why, for Christ's sake, I delight in weaknesses, in insults, in hardships, in persecutions, in difficulties. For when I am weak, then I am strong" (2 Corinthians 12:10).

Personal Growth Tips

Personal Growth Tip #1
FIRST AND FOREMOST:
BE KNOWN FOR YOUR LOVE

There is a hymn with the refrain, "They'll Know We Are Christians by Our Love."[3] Yet, today Christians are often described as "hypocrites", "judgmental", "out-of-touch," and "intolerant." At the same time, most people characterize Jesus as kind and compassionate. Why is this?

Jesus did not judge people. He patiently taught them the way to have a better life and how to go to Heaven. He spoke the truth in love. As Christians we have the same calling. God knew we would need a constant reminder and so He put it in His Word. "Judge not lest ye be judged" (Matthew 7:1).

Do you like it when someone criticizes you? Is your opinion likely to change during an argument or debate? No. These approaches close hearts. They prevent our listener's ability to hear, and to be receptive to what we are trying to tell them. Yet the Bible says, "...faith comes from hearing the message, and the message is heard through the word about Christ" (Romans 10:17).

While our righteous anger over sin and our desire to defend Jesus are well-intentioned, even Jesus did not "defend" himself. The Bible simply says: "...declare the praises of him who called you out of darkness into his wonderful light" (1 Peter 2:9). Speak only of Jesus and what He has done for you.

"By this everyone will know that you are my disciples,
if you love one another" (John 13:35).

Personal Growth Tip #2
CREATE AND PRAY FOR YOUR "PRIORITY LIST"

*"Commit to the L*ORD *whatever you do, and he will
establish your plans" (Proverbs 16:3).*

One of the components to any successful regimen is to be intentional. And
so it is with evangelism. If you are going to be intentional about sharing
your faith, praying for others is the best way to start. After all, it is God
who changes hearts.

Who do you know that is not a Christian? Too many to count? So begin
with a manageable list. Close your eyes right now and ask God to lay the
names of specific people on your heart. Write the names down...maybe
in your Bible. This will be your "Priority List"—approximately five or six
people: friends, family, neighbors, associates, retail clerks, etc.

Establish a regimen. Perhaps, at the beginning of each week, pray for the
salvation of the people on your "Priority List." Ask God to open doors for
you, and others, to witness to them. By all means, continue to share Jesus
in word and deed with those whom God places in your path.

I have my "Priority List" names on my monthly To-do List. This helps me
to stay in touch more regularly—otherwise time races by. I make a point of
finding out what is going on in their lives without an agenda. When I feel
God wants me to "go deeper," I pray for Him to show me the opportunity
and to give me the words.

"Devote yourselves to prayer, being watchful and thankful" (Colossians 4:2).

11

Personal Growth Tip #3
DEVELOP COMPASSION FOR THE LOST

How do we develop compassion for those who do not have a relationship with Christ?

Developing compassion for naysayers, particularly family and friends, can be difficult. Remember that you at one time were also comfortable in your sin. God is using you to model love to soften their hearts. Some hear and believe the first time, others must bottom out.

Praying for others' souls will propel you along the road to sanctification (becoming more like Jesus). As your heart aches more for the unsaved, you will experience increased understanding of God's will for your life. Creating and praying for your "Priority List" (the previous Personal Growth Tip #2) is one way to do this.

Compassion is a key part of our walk with Christ. The definition of compassion is "a feeling of deep sympathy or sorrow for another who is stricken with misfortune, accompanied by a strong desire to alleviate the suffering."[4] The biggest misfortune there could ever be is eternal separation from God!

Compassion is not simply feeling sorry for someone who is suffering; it is taking action to end the suffering. God's compassion for mankind was so great that He sent his only Son to die. Pray to God to move you to action on behalf of unsaved people.

One way I foster compassion for the lost is to envision my unsaved family members and friends crying out to me from Hell, asking me why I didn't try harder to share the gospel message with them. This visual keeps me praying for them, planting seeds, and even boldly asking them what is holding them back from making a decision for Christ.

> *"Therefore, as God's chosen people, holy and dearly loved,*
> *clothe yourselves with compassion, kindness, humility,*
> *gentleness and patience" (Colossians 3:12).*

Personal Growth Tip #4
MEMORIZE AND MEDITATE ON GOD'S WORD

Do you have your "ABC's" and the Pledge of Allegiance memorized? Of course you do! How about advertising jingles? Christmas songs? Then you can memorize scripture too!

"I can do all this through him who gives me strength" (Philippians 4:13).

God desires that we all study and know His Word. We need His Word to guide our daily decisions and to offer encouragement to both Christians and non-Christians. Do not be impressed when others know Scripture—be intentional to do the same!

"Fix these words of mine in your hearts and minds" (Deuteronomy 11:18).

Philippians 4:8 is the first verse I memorized: "...whatever is true, whatever is noble, whatever is right, whatever is pure, whatever is lovely, whatever is admirable—if anything is excellent or praiseworthy—think about such things." At that time, my mind was rapidly cycling through such debilitating thoughts that I was literally unable to function.

I meditated (pondered, reflected) on this verse constantly, uttering it over and over again. I wrote it on an index card, carrying it everywhere and reading it constantly. Ultimately the sword of the Spirit, which is the Word of God, enabled me to rebuke Satan, and to focus on the good of my situation.

"I meditate on your precepts and consider your ways" (Psalm 119:15).

Rick Warren's "Twenty Verses Every Believer Needs to Memorize" is a good place to start. Choose one of the verses and write in on an index card. Then meditate on it to hide it in your heart. Not only does knowing God' Word help you to navigate life in God's will, you are always ready to share it with others.

Personal Growth Tip #5
TAKE A TIME OUT AND CHANGE YOUR APPROACH

Of course you want your brother, aunt, friend, etc. to know Christ! Not only do you pray for them on a regular basis, you touch base with them frequently. You are very well-intentioned when you explain what is wrong with their belief system. You send Christian literature and follow up diligently to inquire whether or not they have read it. You respond rapidly to their Facebook posts, clarifying their misconceptions about God, Jesus, and Christianity.

There is nothing wrong with your zeal, but there becomes a point where you are definitely hurting and not helping the situation. Give it a rest. Even if this advice seems contradictory to The Great Commission, it is not. Remember, you are not doing the convincing. It's the Holy Spirit that is doing the convicting. Leave room for the Holy Spirit to work.

Change your approach: pray that God will change *you*. Of course, continue to pray for your friend/loved one, but keep in mind God is on the job. After you have "laid off" the preaching for a while, begin to take an honest, non-judgmental interest in your friend/loved one's belief system. Ask sincere questions about how they developed their conclusions. Questions make people think; forcing your faith will drive them away. It sounds cliché, but God gave us two ears to hear, one mouth to talk.

Continue to pray that God would use other Christians to influence them. Keep in touch, and ask personal details about their life. Of course plant a few seeds here and there. As you demonstrate that you are truly interested in them and that you don't have an agenda, their defenses will drop and they may even ask you about your beliefs. Refer to Personal Growth Tip #1—Let Them Know We Are Christians by Our Love (not by our harassment).

"So in everything, do to others what you would
have them do to you…" (Matthew 7:12).

Personal Growth Tip #6
BEWARE!
"BEING A GOOD EXAMPLE" IS NOT ENOUGH

From time to time I hear the comment, "I just lead my life as a good example so others will notice." While this thought is well-intentioned, it is a passive approach to Christianity. Yes, people may notice you are nice and helpful, and even comment on it, but will they ask why? Probably not. There are many friendly, generous people out there—a lot of them unchurched!

Consider this comment by staunch atheist, Penn Jillette (magician in the team Penn & Teller). "How much do you have to hate somebody to believe everlasting life is possible and not tell them that? If I believe beyond a shadow of a doubt that a truck was coming at you and you didn't believe it, there is a certain point where I would tackle you. And this is way more important."[5]

"Love" is an action word! Don't be just well-intentioned: be proactive to love in word and deed. Let's go make disciples by telling others what it means to have a personal relationship with Christ!

> *"What good is it, my brothers and sisters, if someone claims to have faith but has no deeds?" (James 2:14).*

What people will notice is if you profess to be a Christian and your life doesn't match up. Study the Bible, fellowship with other believers, and pray to be in God's will so that as you apply your Christian knowledge you will be a testament to the Holy One.

> *"If I speak in the tongues of men or of angels, but do not have love, I am only a resounding gong or a clanging cymbal" (1 Corinthians 13:1).*

Super Simple Tips

#1 Let Others See You Reading Your Bible
#2 Use the Phrase "Good Lord Willing"
#3 Put a Bible Verse on Your Bumper
#4 Acknowledge Compliments by Giving God the Glory
#5 Wear Your Witness
#6 Give a Gospel Tract
#7 Display God's Wisdom on the Wall
#8 Tune In to Christian Radio
#9 Sign Off with Scripture

Super Simple Tip #1
LET OTHERS SEE YOU READING YOUR BIBLE

Do you have preferred locations to read and study your Bible? I do! In addition to church and Bible Study, I favor reading the Bible in my home office in the early morning hours and while waiting in my car (during my sons' sports activities). While it is good that I am in the Word, I am failing to model reading the Bible to my own family, let alone unchurched people!

Of course it's okay to continue reading the Bible in private. Simply expand your locations so that others may observe you. For example: on the plane, in your office or your employer's cafeteria, at school, etc. Read at a coffee shop—better yet, hold a Bible study there! Whether you realize it or not, people are watching. Eventually you will get some questions/comments.

If someone asks you why you are reading the Bible, a possible response is, "I'm trying to work through an issue. Did you know that the Bible is an acronym for "Best Instructions Before Leaving Earth"?

Super Simple Tip #2
USE THE PHRASE "GOOD LORD WILLING'

When you speak about a future activity, include the phrase "Good Lord Willing." For example, "Good Lord willing, our family is camping in Yosemite this summer." Or "We plan to buy a house this year, Good Lord willing." This phrase demonstrates that you recognize you are not ultimately in control of your life, and it may cause your listener to do the same.

This phrase is used so rarely, chances are your listener will contemplate its meaning even after your conversation is over. If you type "GLW" in texts or emails, you are certain to get a question. The phrase "Good Lord Willing" could become a natural segue for you to share the gospel.

"Why, you do not even know what will happen tomorrow...Instead, you ought to say, 'If it is the Lord's will, we will live and do this or that'"
(James 4:14-15).

Super Simple Tip #3
PUT A BIBLE VERSE ON YOUR BUMPER

Many people use their car for marketing. Why not? Sometimes it seems like we are in our car all day. While you are sitting in gridlock and at traffic lights, why not give the person behind you the blessing of a Bible verse? Imagine the countless people who will read that scripture on your car and unknowingly have their hearts impacted! Isaiah 55:11 reminds us that His Word does not return void (Biblical Reassurance Tip #4).

There are a large variety of inexpensive Bible Verse bumper stickers available online. Why not order a few extras for your friends? The verse on my bumper is, "For God did not send his Son into the world to condemn the world, but to save the world through Him" (John 3:17). I shy away from using John 3:16 because, as Pastor and Evangelist Greg Laurie says, "Why tell someone the good news unless they know the bad news first?"

Super Simple Tip #4
ACKNOWLEDGE COMPLIMENTS
BY GIVING GOD THE GLORY

Giving Compliments

When paying a compliment, use verbiage that indicates the talent is from God. For example, "God has gifted you with such a beautiful voice," or "God gave you that passion for repairing automobile engines and He has a plan for you."

Employ this same concept when speaking in the third person. "God has gifted Pastor Mark with the ability to make great analogies and illustrations to help us understand God's Word." "Jana's gift from God is wisdom," or "Laura used her God-given talent of hospitality to host a wonderful Christmas party."

When you give the glory to God, this illustrates that talents are from the Creator, and not from the person themselves. Of course, the individual has probably worked hard to hone their skills.

Receiving Compliments

When someone pays you a compliment, always start with a simple "thank you." Then immediately give God the glory. For example, if a parent says, "I'm so glad that you are my child's teacher."

A good response could be, "Thank you. I'm fortunate God has given me the skills to work in a profession I enjoy."

Super Simple Tip #5
WEAR YOUR WITNESS

When you wear t-shirts or caps with Christian text, they will be noticed. A couple examples I have seen include "He is Risen" and "Jesus Saves Bro."

Speaking from experience, when you wear Christian clothes you will get "high fives" from other Christians, and you will notice strangers looking at you a little longer than normal. You have planted or watered a seed! Recently a man at a gas station looked at my shirt and shared how God was working in his life. Wearing your witness also keeps you accountable to live a godly life in your daily walk.

Perhaps you received a t-shirt when you volunteered at Vacation Bible School. Continue to wear that shirt even after VBS is over. A friend of mine wears her VBS t-shirts when she works as a playground supervisor. Many students recognize her shirts and make comments or about it. God has opened this avenue for her to be an incredible witness.

Do you wear jewelry with any Christian significance? When someone notices it, say something like, "This [necklace, pin, etc.] reminds me of the most important decision of my life: when I became a Christian by claiming Jesus as my Lord and Savior."

Hosting and/or attending jewelry parties on behalf of Christian organizations is also a fun avenue to "go make disciples." For example, Purpose Jewelry provides sustainable employment for survivors of trafficking:

www.purposejewelry.org

Super Simple Tip #6
GIVE A GOSPEL TRACT

Many religious organizations, as well as Christians, hand out tracts (pamphlets) at public places such as airports and college campuses. Generally speaking, tracts are used more to disseminate the gospel than to create individual relationships. Yet there are countless testimonies of how these gospel tracts have not only saved spiritual lives, but physical lives.

My pastor's wife uses "Are You a Good Person?" tracts available from <u>www.livingwaters.com</u>. Her husband recommends leaving a tract, along with a good tip (not huge, but a little more than generally accepted) when you eat at sit-down restaurants.

Coffee shops, ice cream and frozen yogurt stores, etc. often have tip jars at the cash register. Why not be a little extra generous and drop in a dollar and a tract?

You can place tracts in hospital waiting rooms or chapels; this gospel message may be just what someone reaches for when searching for comfort and hope. Often hospitals and care facilities have book carts that will accept books and tracts to make available for their patients.

Super Simple Tip #7
DISPLAY GOD'S WISDOM ON THE WALL

Consider displaying a Bible verse in your home, office, classroom, etc. Posting God's Word for all to see is a wonderful way to instill God's wisdom in the hearts and minds of any who read it. Just one or two scriptures located in high-traffic areas work best.

A popular verse to display is "But as for me and my household, we will serve the Lord" (Joshua 24:15). A friend of ours has a sign in his home above the door that reads: "You Are Now Entering the Mission Field." I have teen boys and have posted, "Do not be misled: 'Bad company corrupts good character'" (1 Corinthians 15:33). Below this verse I added, "If you want to soar like an eagle, then don't hang out with the turkeys." (No offense to turkeys!)

Create your own simple or innovative masterpiece, or google "Christian wall decals" for a myriad of verses in sizes and styles to fit any décor.

"Tie them as symbols on your hands and bind them
on your foreheads" (Deuteronomy 6:8).

Super Simple Tip #8
TUNE IN TO CHRISTIAN RADIO

Some time ago a friend recommended a Christian radio station and I am hooked! The station I listen to predominantly plays pre-recorded sermons. Whether I tune in for five minutes or catch the whole program, I am getting great Bible teaching. Amazingly, the teaching always seems to be pertinent to my life.

My pastor suggests "snacking" on God's Word throughout the day by having Bibles and devotionals throughout the house, in your car, etc. Christian radio is a great way to "snack." And each time I listen there seem to be some nuggets I can share with others that day.

You may wonder: How is tuning into Christian radio a practical evangelism tip? The more time you invest in God's Word, the more you crave God's Word. And, if you are humble and willing, the more God will change you from the inside out. God's priorities will become your priorities, and one of those priorities is sharing the gospel. As you consistently listen, study, and reflect on Scripture, you will learn to love others as Jesus did and offer them godly wisdom instead of worldly wisdom. One hour on Sunday is not going to cut it.

Play Christian radio (and music) at home, too. Many years ago, my friend had a contractor doing some work in her home. Approximately a year later, she received a letter from him. He wrote to tell her that at the time his wife had been dying from cancer and it was her music that helped him make it through.

My friend did take the opportunity to follow up and share the gospel with him. If you are willing, God will use you!

Super Simple Tip #9
SIGN OFF WITH SCRIPTURE

We send and receive countless emails per day. Why not include a Bible verse at the end of your message? Not only will it identify you as a Christian, it will be a blessing to many. For those who don't like it…that's because it's the truth permeating their heart!

It is very simple to create an email signature:

1. Open a new message and click on "Insert Heading".
2. Click "Signature" and then click "Signatures."
3. On the E-mail Signature tab, click New.
4. Type a name for the signature, and then click OK.
5. In the Edit signature box, type the text that you want to include in the signature.
6. To format the text, select the text, and then use the style and formatting buttons to select the options you prefer.

Once you have created an email signature, your Bible verse will automatically be sent when you create a new email message. Now the challenge becomes: will you keep that verse on every email you send? Or will you delete it from specific messages (i.e., when communicating with an atheist friend or prospective employer)?

Often-Forgotten Tips

Often-Forgotten Tip #1
STOCKPILE WISDOM

First thing in the morning, do you rush to exercise, check emails, or analyze your portfolio? Before long it's a race against time to get yourself (and maybe the kids) ready and out the door. Reading the Bible at the beginning of the day seems impossible.

As we get out of bed, C.S. Lewis in *Mere Christianity* says, "...all your wishes and hopes for the day rush at you like wild animals." "One reason we read the Bible is so that we are not subject to living the day out of haste but rather out of calm. We remember the shortness of life, the eternality of heaven..."[6]

Your Father in Heaven is anxious to interact with you. He would be ecstatic with three dedicated minutes in the morning compared to nothing. And when you meet with Him through reading his Word, he will communicate his priorities specifically for you and give you the wisdom to move forward.

"Bible reading is stored energy, stockpiled emotional and psychological capital. We stay afloat throughout the day by making moment-by-moment withdrawals from that vast reservoir."[v] If we don't read the Bible first thing in the morning, our reservoirs will not be to full capacity. We want our godly wisdom to overflow throughout the day to ourselves and others.

One idea is to read from Proverbs each day. Proverbs has thirty-one chapters: one for each day of the month. Imagine the godly wisdom you (or your kids) could gain and apply! Listen to a Chapter on Bible Gateway's app at home or in the car. Putting on the full armor of God at the beginning of the day makes us less likely to fall prey to the priorities of the world.

"Do not conform to the pattern of this world, but be transformed by the renewing of your mind. Then you will be able to test and approve what God's will is—his good, pleasing and perfect will" (Romans 12:2).

Often-Forgotten Tip #2
MAKE YOUR HOME A MISSION FIELD

We can get so wrapped up "doing God's work" outside the home that we forget the importance of influencing those with whom we live. Our home is also a mission field!

If you claim to be a Christian, the people with whom you live (roommates, parents, spouse, children) will hold you to a higher standard. This is especially challenging at home where we "let it all hang out." Yet it is an opportunity to become more Christ-like. Seek God's guidance moment by moment to learn to live in his will.

> *"No temptation has overtaken you except what is common to mankind. And God is faithful; he will not let you be tempted beyond what you can bear. But when you are tempted, he will also provide a way out so that you can endure it" (1 Corinthians 10:13).*

If you live with a non-Christian, you cannot "make" them a Christian. Do not come on too strong. However, here is what you can do: 1) desire and allow God to change you; and 2) pray for God to soften the heart of the non-Christian. God is on the job! In God's perfect timing you will see evidence of change.

When you live with someone, you become familiar with their strengths and weaknesses. Because Satan is divisive, he will tempt us to focus on the weaknesses. Instead, write down all of the things you appreciate about the other person and refer to this list whenever you begin developing a bad attitude toward that person.

> *"A new command I give you: Love one another. As I have loved you, so you must love one another" (John 13:34).*

Often-Forgotten Tip #3
PRAY IN PUBLIC

Before Eating

Whether you are eating a meal in a restaurant, having coffee with a friend, or enjoying a picnic at the park, giving God thanks before you eat is a great way to reflect on his provision. When you pray in public, bowing your head or holding hands...others notice! Praise God that we still have this freedom!

Even if you are dining with unchurched people, before eating ask if anyone minds if you say a short prayer. Chances are you will never be turned down...even when invited to a non-Christian's home. Most people really like it!

Holding a Bible Study, prayer group, or mentoring session at a park, coffee shop, restaurant, etc. is also a good way to witness.

During a Conversation

If you are talking with someone and they share a difficulty with you, ask them if you can pray for them immediately.

The vast majority of people will say yes. My pastor indicated that no one, Christian or otherwise, has ever turned him down. Only one person has declined my offer to pray for them right then and there (a good friend no less)!

In my experience non-Christians seem to be the most grateful for these immediate prayers. Many of them have never known the peace of being in God's presence. Additionally, you are modeling that prayer, contrary to what many believe, can be done anytime, anywhere, and is just like talking to a friend.

> *"But whoever disowns me before others, I will disown*
> *before my Father in heaven" (Matthew 10:33).*

Often-Forgotten Tip #4
TAKE INITIATIVE

Have you ever sent a well-intentioned message like this: "I'll be praying for you; let me know how I can help?"

That is not helping. First of all, the individual may not even know what kind of help they need. And now you are making them ask for help, which many people are tentative to do.

Here are a couple examples of how some non-Christians took initiative to help our family:

- We had a pile of gravel in our driveway and the next door neighbor sauntered over with a shovel, a smile, and said, "What are we waiting for?"
- After we had our first baby (overwhelmed and sleep-deprived), a girl friend called and said she was coming over on Saturday night to watch our son so we could take a break.

At the time, it would never have dawned on us to ask for help in these situations, or frankly, that anyone would want to help us in these ways. Yet these gestures continue to leave an impression today, and in fact have propelled us to do the same.

Simply call someone and let them know when and what you would like to do for them. Before they hesitate and say, "Oh, that's okay, you don't have to..." be sure you tell them that you really want to help because the blessing is yours. Perhaps they will accept your offer or clarify something else you can do. Regardless, they will recognize that you cared enough to take initiative and mastermind the details. Love is an action word. Let them know that we are Christians by our love.

"Carry each other's burdens, and in this way you will fulfill the law of Christ" (Galatians 6:2).

Often-Forgotten Tip #5
ENCOURAGE THOSE ON THE FRONT LINES

Are you more productive when people recognize you and thank you for whatever it is that you do? Of course! It is no different for those in the ministry. Take a little time to encourage these people and energize them to continue "making disciples of all nations."

> *"And let us consider how we may spur one another on*
> *toward love and good deeds" (Hebrews 10:24).*

Your Pastor Have you ever stopped to consider how many complaints pastors receive? Discouragement is one of the main reasons talented pastors quit.

A compliment brings such encouragement! Jot a note, send an email, or tell your pastor in person. Share something specific, for example, "Thanks for taking the time to write those devotionals on the back of the sermon notes--they are really helping me grow" or "That was a great Easter service, our guests are regulars now."

Missionaries These Christian warriors follow God's calling to leave everything they know behind and relocate to strange lands. Can you imagine how welcome a care package, a little taste of home, would be?

On your own, or with your Bible Study group, adopt a missionary you know or one that your church supports. Send care packages for Christmas and birthdays. One Christmas our group emailed a missionary family in Cambodia asking for gift ideas. Sheepishly the father told us they would love some Starbucks coffee beans!

Anytime throughout the year, send a photo and a simple card letting them know you are praying for them. It will be desperately needed encouragement. Remembering missionary kids with a gift on their birthday or Christmas not only blesses the child but their parents, too.

Gift Tips

Gift Tip #1
RECOMMEND THESE BOOKS

Safely Home by Randy Alcorn is a wonderful book that, once read, begs the question, "Why am I afraid to share the gospel?" The story takes place in modern-day China and chronicles the shocking twenty-year reunion of two Harvard graduates.

While this novel is fictional, the details about the persecution of the Chinese Christians are accurate. *Safely Home* allows the reader a glimpse into the dangerous lifestyle Chinese Christians willingly accept in order to worship and share Jesus Christ. It won the Gold Medallion Book Award for evangelical literature.

Case for Christ is written by Lee Strobel, a former atheist. This bestseller chronicles Strobel's quest to prove whether Jesus of Nazareth is the Son of God.

Strobel searches for credible evidence by cross-examining experts in various fields of Biblical studies. *Case for Christ* is a good read for all Christians in order to better defend their faith. This book is also a good gift for atheists; their thinking will be challenged by the facts Lee uncovers.

How You Can Be Sure That You Will Spend Eternity With God by Erwin Lutzer is the book I purchased at the event where I heard the gospel message. Shortly after reading it I gave my life to the Lord. Since many people become Christians because they do not want to go to hell, this book can provide the evidence they need to make a decision for Christ.

Gift Tip #2
GIVE A TIMELESS GIFT

Gift a Bible

Buy a few Bibles to have on hand to give as gifts. When you are speaking to someone and it's evident they are in distress, ask if they own a Bible. Most times they do not (in my experience). Let them know you would like to give them one and follow up in a few days.

Select a version that you like. I gift *START! The Bible for New Believers.* Greg Laurie is the general editor. He has included the Plan of Salvation and his Secrets to Spiritual Success at the front of the book. Always recommend reading the Gospel of John first, since this book demonstrates that Jesus is the Son of God.

Recommend an App

Here are some excellent free resources for most electronic devices.

- www.biblegateway.com Scripture available in more than 70 languages and 180 versions. Search and compare passages in multiple Bible translations. Opt to receive daily devotionals or verses of the day.
- www.faithcomesbyhearing.com The Bible in every translated language.
- www.Bible.isThe Bible in 1668 languages and the JESUS Film.

Send Bibles to Persecuted Believers

Despite incredible risk, many persecuted believers have been waiting years to own their own Bible. Send them one for $6. This ministry is offered through Voice of the Martyrs at www.biblesunbound.com

Gift an "Our Daily Bread" Booklet

These pocket-sized booklets include a Bible passage and a relevant article for each day of the year. Many churches offer them free of charge. Carry an extra to give away.

Gift Tip #3
EXTEND ETERNAL ENTERTAINMENT

We all love a really good movie, and the following films are outstanding. Each played on the big screen and demonstrates how God transforms lives. They are appropriate for all ages. Have a few of these DVDs on hand for gifts. Purchase them inexpensively on Amazon.

Courageous
A policeman is attempting to endure the tragic death of his daughter.

Facing the Giants
Everyone will love this film about an underdog high school football team and its struggling coach. Subthemes include financial and infertility issues. Gift this DVD to any coach as a way of saying thanks at the end of a season.

Fireproof
Kirk Cameron portrays a firefighter ready to give up on his marriage.

God's Not Dead
A college student must choose between his belief in God or fail a course. This film contains the gospel message verbatim!

War Room
A family, who appears to be living the "American Dream," is inwardly falling apart.

How about hosting a movie night? Invite a few people, order a pizza, and watch any of these films. Who said evangelizing couldn't be fun?

Financial Tips

#1 Tithe Consistently

#2 Sponsor a Child in Jesus' Name

#3 Take the Bible to Our Troops

#4 Stop Sighing

Financial Tip #1
TITHE CONSISTENTLY

"For where your treasure is, there your heart will be also" (Matthew 6:21).

Tithing is a form of evangelism. God doesn't need your money...His purpose will be accomplished whether or not you choose to participate. However, someone needs to pay for the electricity so the lights will be on at church!

Giving "your" hard-earned money can be very difficult. Yet your abilities and employment are gifts from God. Whether you are young or old, earn a lot or a little, are paid regularly or sporadically, God's people are called to tithe. Tithing helps you to live by faith.

> *"...Remember the Lord your God, for it is he who gives you the ability to produce wealth" (Deuteronomy 8:18).*

When you trust God for adequate provision and are obedient to tithe, He will transform your attitude about the purpose for your money. You will become grateful for the eternal benefits your tithing provides. However, when it comes to giving, God's priority is your heart.

> *"Each of you should give what you have decided in your heart to give, not reluctantly or under compulsion, for God loves a cheerful giver" (2 Corinthians 9:7).*

Commit to the tithing method that keeps you consistent. One suggestion is to set up automatic transfer on the first of the month. Three benefits include: 1) you are giving God your best--your "first fruits" as was done in the Old Testament; 2) it keeps you consistent; and 3) it helps eliminate the temptation to decrease your giving for months when cash seems especially tight.

> *"Whoever sows sparingly will also reap sparingly, and whoever sows generously will also reap generously" (2 Corinthians 9:6).*

Financial Tip #2
SPONSOR A CHILD IN JESUS' NAME

"Religion that God our Father accepts as pure and faultless is this: to look after widows and orphans in their distress" (James 1:27).

Did you know that you can sponsor a child in Jesus' name for about $1 per day? Christian organizations such as World Vision and Compassion International make this possible. Since adoption may not be viable for most people, this is the next best thing!

Your donation will be used to provide necessities such as seeds to plant and sustain food, clean drinking water, and educational materials. Your sponsored child will also be taught about their value to Jesus and how to have a personal relationship with him.

If you desire, you can choose your child's age, gender, and country of residence. You will receive photos and updates. You can be as involved as you want to be. Some people even visit their sponsored child!

www.worldvision.org
www.compassioninternational.org

Financial Tip #3
TAKE THE BIBLE TO OUR TROOPS

What better gift can we give our men and women in uniform than God's Word? They risk their lives for our freedom here on earth; let us equip them for eternity!

> *"Greater love has no one than this: to lay down*
> *one's life for one's friends" (John 15:13).*

Consider providing troops with the Military BibleStick. It is a rugged digital audio player, about the size of a pack of gum, and fits into uniform pockets. It's pre-loaded with a dramatized recording of the entire New Testament and selected Psalms.

www.militarybiblestick.com

The Military BibleStick Outreach brings the pure Word of God to our troops while on (and preparing for) deployment. BibleSticks are provided to our troops at no cost to them through military chaplains. The troops must put in requests and currently there are not enough to go around. $50 provides BibleSticks for two troops, yet any amount helps.

Financial Tip #4
STOP SIGHING

Do you ever feel frustrated when you discover a Christian cause to which you would like to contribute, but another monthly deduction is just not feasible?

Here is a perfect solution: make a small one-time donation! Organizations mean it when they say, "Any amount helps." Instead of sighing and throwing literature in the trash, give five or ten dollars. If one hundred of us gave ten dollars each, that would be one thousand dollars!

Use this tip not only to alleviate future guilt—make a difference today! Give to a cause of your choice or to one of the following:

Alliance Defending Freedom www.adflegal.org
Pacific Justice Institute www.pacificjustice.org
Both advocate for Christians to freely live out their faith

Campus Crusade for Christ www.cru.org
Brings the gospel to all nations

Harvest America www.harvestamerica.org
Large-scale public evangelistic events: Harvest Crusades

International Justice Mission www.ijm.org
Provides justice for the poor in developing countries in Jesus' name

Samaritan's Purse www.samaritanspurse.org
Aids the world's poor, sick, and suffering in Jesus' name

Voice of the Martyrs www.persecution.com
Dedicated to assisting persecuted Christians worldwide

Young Life www.younglife.org
Introduces adolescents around the globe to Jesus Christ

Critical Conversation Tips

#1 Clarify Christianity v. Religion

#2 Master a Simple Gospel Message

#3 Tell Your Testimony in 30 Seconds

#4 Ask Questions and Actively Listen

#5 Anticipate Common Objections by Using the Bible as the Authority

#6 Never Assume Someone is Saved: Ask If They Have a Personal Relationship with Jesus

Critical Conversation Tip #1
CLARIFY CHRISTIANITY V. RELIGION

Many people take issue with "organized religion." A few points for clarification:

- Religion is man-made.
- Christianity is not a religion...it is a relationship with Jesus Christ.
- Religion focuses on being "good enough" or "poor enough." When do you know if you've done enough?
- It is not what we do that makes us Christians. It's what Jesus did. When He died on the cross, Jesus cried, "It is finished!"
- Jesus rose from the dead three days later. He is alive! We serve a risen Savior. Which other "religions" can make this claim?

Critical Conversation Tip #2
MASTER A SIMPLE GOSPEL MESSAGE

If you are a Christian, then you have responded affirmatively to the gospel message, also known as the "good news". You have claimed Jesus as your Lord and Savior. You are also known as "saved" or "born again." This means that the power of the Holy Spirit resides in you. Therefore you are qualified to share the gospel. A missionary taught me the following method shortly after I became a Christian.

Gospel Share--Memorize Four Words:
"God, Man, God, Man"

- *God is perfect*
- *Man is a sinner (separated from God)*
- *God sent Jesus as a free gift to be our sin sacrifice*
- *Man chooses whether to accept or reject the gift (Jesus)*

After sharing, ask your listener if they would like to accept the gift of Jesus as their Lord and Savior.

If they say No. 1) Listen to their logic and thank them for allowing you to share. God's timing prevails and the Holy Spirit will continue to work in their heart. Gently remind them that time is of the essence since no one knows what tomorrow brings. Continue the relationship.

If they say Yes. 1) Lead them in a basic prayer acknowledging Jesus as the Son of God and stating their desire to repent from their sins and to begin to live for Christ. 2) Hug them and instruct them to tell someone about their decision before the end of the day. 3) Get them a Bible, recommend a church, and advise them to join a Bible study. Coordinate a few new-Christian mentoring sessions if possible.

Critical Conversation Tip #3
TELL YOUR TESTIMONY IN THIRTY SECONDS

Your testimony is your conversion experience: how you became a Christian ("saved;" "born again" etc.). One of the simplest ways to share your testimony is to use the "God, Man, God, Man" Gospel Share method (see previous tip) and add two details: 1) the date of your conversion (sometimes this is a process that occurs over a period of time); and a specific difference that you experienced shortly after you were born again.

Practice your testimony until it rolls comfortably off your tongue. Speak in everyday language because "Christianese" turns people off. Use a stopwatch to limit your testimony to the salient facts. You never know when God will place someone in your path and thirty seconds may be all the time you have.

> *Your Testimony =*
> *Gospel Share (previous tip)*
> *And Add Two Details: 1) Date 2) Difference*

- **God** *is perfect*
- **Man** *is a sinner (separated from God)*
- **God** *sent Jesus as a free gift to be our sin sacrifice*
- **Man** *chooses whether to accept or reject the gift (Jesus)*
- **Date** *date/timeframe you became a Christian*
- **Difference:** *a specific difference you experienced after your conversion*

Sample 30-Second Testimony

"Even though I went to church most of my life, I didn't become a Christian until after I had kids. I already knew God was perfect, and that since I'm not perfect I'm a sinner like everyone else. What I've since learned is that our sin separates us from God, and that's why Jesus had to die, to be our sin sacrifice. But God created Man with free will to accept or reject that. When I claimed Christ as my Lord and Savior, one big change I noticed was that taking the Lord's name in vain felt wrong."

Critical Conversation Tip #4
ASK QUESTIONS AND ACTIVELY LISTEN

The best method to engage in a conversation is to ask questions. People have to think when they answer a question. When we drone on and on it's easy to tune out. Yes, this tip is similar to Personal Growth Tip #5, but many of us need the reminder to listen instead of to speak.

When you ask a question, you must honestly be interested in what the other has to say. Shut off your phone, make eye contact, and actively listen by processing what they are saying and asking clarifying questions. Do not try to formulate a response while they are talking. Try to understand their vantage point.

As with all communication, listening and understanding is the key. God equipped us for success by giving us two ears and just one mouth. Here are a few good questions include:

- *Have you ever heard the gospel message?*
- *What do you think happens when you die?*
- *Do you have a religious preference?*
- *What is your perspective on Jesus?*
- *Do you believe in Heaven and Hell?*
- *What do you think about the Cross? Christmas? Easter?*

It is fascinating to hear how others' belief systems have been formulated. Both parties usually have misconceptions about the other's point-of-view, so these can be clarified in a positive and non-threatening way. However, if the conversation morphs into a debate, this is not evangelism. Nobody wins. If this occurs, simply agree to disagree.

Critical Conversation Tip #5
ANTICIPATE COMMON OBJECTIONS BY USING THE BIBLE AS THE AUTHORITY

Listed below are some of the common objections folks like to use for "not buying into" Christianity. This list of objections is not comprehensive—*Everyday Evangelism* is not an Apologetics manual. In any discussion focus on the gospel—good news—of Jesus Christ and what a relationship with Jesus has done for you.

If these topics arise, discuss them only if you can do so without debating. Preface your responses with "the Bible says" instead of "I think." This establishes God as the authority. However, do so as it says in 1 Peter 3:15: "with gentleness and respect."

1. **Jesus was just a man (and/or prophet).**

    "...these are written that you may believe that Jesus is the Messiah, the Son of God, and that by believing you may have life in his name" (John 20:31).

    Additional proof exists in that Jesus had a large number of eyewitnesses after his resurrection.

    "...he appeared to Cephas, and then to the Twelve. After that, he appeared to more than five hundred of the brothers and sisters at the same time...Then he appeared to James, then to all the apostles, and last of all he appeared to me..." (1 Corinthians 15:5-7).

2. **There are many ways to heaven.**

    "Jesus answered, I am the way and the truth and the life. No one comes to the Father except through me" (John 14:6).

3. **I am not a sinner.**

    "...for all have sinned and fall short of the glory of God" (Romans 3:23).

Most people will agree that God is perfect and man is imperfect. Explain that this is the very essence of why we need Jesus—to bridge the gap so that we do not have to be separated from God.

God also helps us to understand our sin through the Ten Commandments—it is not possible for anyone to keep them all. Have you ever taken pencils or other supplies from the office? Then you are a thief. Have you told someone their outfit was flattering when it wasn't? Then you are a liar.

4. **There is no such thing as Hell.**

> *"The wicked shall be turned into hell and all the nations that forget God" (Psalm 9:17).*[7]

> *"Just as people are destined to die once, and after that to face judgment..." (Hebrews 9:27-28).*

5. **I can't believe in a God who would send people to hell.**

> *"For God so loved the world that he gave his one and only Son, that whoever believes in him shall not perish but have eternal life" (John 3:16).*

This hallmark verse of Christianity illustrates that God does not desire for anyone to go to Hell—that's why he allowed his One and Only Son to be sacrificed! Yet God does not force himself on us; he created us with free will. If we choose not to align ourselves with God on earth, we are doing the same for eternity. And that's the definition of hell--eternal separation from God.

> *"For God did not send his Son into the world to condemn the world, but to save the world through him. Whoever believes in him is not condemned, but whoever does not believe stands condemned already because they have not believed in the name of God's one and only Son" (John 3:17-18).*

6. **How would a God who is good allow such terrible things to happen?**

> *"I have told you these things, so that in me you may have peace. In this world you will have trouble. But take heart! I have overcome the world" (John 16:33).*

Scripture tells us that life will be tough, but this was not God's plan for the world. He created a perfect place. Mankind chose to ignore God's instructions by giving into Satan's temptations. This is when sin entered the world—when the world became "fallen." Satan is "prince," or god, of this fallen world for a time.

> *"The god of this age has blinded the minds of unbelievers, so that they cannot see the light of the gospel that displays the glory of Christ, who is the image of God" (2 Corinthians 4:4).*

Even though Satan rules the Earth, God is so good that the hardships He allows in our lives are opportunities to turn to Him for grace and peace. Even in Revelation God does not release His wrath all at one—in his infinite love and patience he continues to extend opportunities for salvation until the very end.

Only a good Creator would allow us to choose whether or not to worship him. God did not create robots—he gave us free will to decide whether or not to claim Jesus as our Lord and Savior.

> *"The fear of the LORD leads to life; then one rests content, untouched by trouble" (Proverbs 19:23).*

Critical Conversation #6
NEVER ASSUME ANYONE IS SAVED: ASK IF THEY HAVE A PERSONAL RELATIONSHIP WITH JESUS

Have you ever asked anyone if they have a personal relationship with Jesus Christ?

Chances are you've heard something along these lines: "Well, I haven't been going to church for a while," or "I just started going to church again." Or possibly, "I've been baptized," or "I do pray to God." These responses generally indicate the person is not a Christian. He or she does not understand that we cannot earn salvation by our own efforts ("works"). Jesus took care of our salvation on the cross; the only thing we have to do is, in faith, accept His gift.

> *"This righteousness is given through faith in Jesus Christ to all who believe" (Romans 3:22).*

Rather than condemning the non-Christian, follow up with this question: "What was one of the changes you experienced when you accepted Jesus as Lord of your life?" You may get a blank stare. This could be the perfect opportunity to share your 30-Second Testimony (Critical Conversation Tip #3). Be sure to highlight a change you experienced once you became infused with the Holy Spirit.

> *"...If anyone is in Christ, the new creation has come: The old has gone, the new is here!" (2 Corinthians 5:17).*

On a final note, be wary when people say "I've always been a Christian." No one is born a Christian; we have all been born into sin. Just because your parents are Christians or because you were born in America, etc., does not make you a Christian. Jesus said, "Very truly I tell you, no one can enter the kingdom of God unless they are born of water and the Spirit" (John 3:4-5).

Relational Tips

Relational Tip #1
MIRROR CHRIST ON SOCIAL MEDIA

With three-quarters of Americans online using social media,[8] it has a huge capacity to reach people for Christ. However, if not used in God's will, social media can further the chasm between believers and non-believers.

If you identify yourself as a Christian, it is very important that your online presence supports this. For example:

- Refrain from slander and gossip about anyone such as acquaintances, political figures, and celebrities;
- Post photos with modest clothing and wholesome activities;
- Abstain from commenting about divisive subjects such as politics and religion.

If you remain in God's will on social media, you can do a lot of good. Conduct your own research on how best to evangelize on your preferred social medium. Since Facebook is the most popular social media site as of the printing of this book, here are a few tips to use on Facebook:[9]

- "Like" your church and post upcoming Special Events;
- Post encouraging Scripture verses, devotionals, songs, etc.;
- Type a prayer directly to anyone who lists a concern or need;
- Share your testimony and how your life has changed since accepting Jesus as your Lord and Savior;
- Be real/be humble;
- List things or people you are thankful for;
- Name some of the ways that you've been blessed recently;
- When you are going through a tough time, or in response to the growing atrocities in our world, post ways that your relationship with God gives you peace;
- Locate old classmates, former co-workers, etc. and "friend" them. Develop relationships with them and share Christ.

Relational Tip #2
FIND A NEW FACE AT CHURCH

Most churches have designated areas in which to socialize before and after service. Instead of zeroing in on friends, find someone you don't know. Approach them and introduce yourself. Ask how long they have been attending and take a few minutes to get to know them. Explain the best way for them to get connected at your church. If possible, introduce them to anyone you recognize in the vicinity.

If your church reserves a few minutes during service to introduce yourself to those around you, remember the name of the person sitting next to you. As everyone is rushing out, say "It was nice to meet you {name}. Have a great week!" In some cases you will strike up a conversation. Asking them how long they have been attending your church is always a great icebreaker. Regardless, people are more apt to return if a church is friendly and if someone makes a point to speak to them.

If you strike up a conversation with someone new at church, God may prompt you to invite them to your home that afternoon. Or to your Bible Study. Get their name and phone number and take it from there. What a simple way to "let them know we are Christians by our love."

"Do not forget to show hospitality to strangers, for by so doing some people have shown hospitality to angels without knowing it" (Hebrews 13:2).

Relational Tip #3
INTRODUCE YOURSELF TO A NEIGHBOR

Have you seen "For Sale" signs in your neighborhood with no clue as to who even lives there? I'm certainly guilty as charged! When my kids were young I knew my neighbors' names since I was outside all the time. Now I just pull into my garage and shut the door behind me like everyone else.

God intentionally placed our neighbors near us for a reason. How hard would it be for me to walk over to a neighbor's house and introduce myself? It would also be a perfect opportunity to mention my church and leave one of my church's business cards (Invitation Tip #2)! Even small gestures like this make a big difference. "They'll know we are Christians by our love."

Relational Tip #4
BE A GOOD SAMARITAN

Have you ever spotted a homeless person and altered your path in order to avoid them? (I have.) Isn't that what the priest and the Levite did in the parable of the Good Samaritan?

> *"Give to the one who begs from you, and do not refuse the one who would borrow from you"* (Matthew 5:42).

Jesus loved the outcasts. We can do the same by respecting homeless people, who are also created in God's image. Greet them with a pleasant hello, introduce yourself and ask their name. Then call them by name. How long do you think it has been since they've heard their name spoken aloud? Have a brief conversation. What a gift you have given them to acknowledge them as a human being versus acting as though they were invisible!

> *"Is it not to share your food with the hungry and to provide the poor wanderer with shelter—when you see the naked, to clothe them, and not to turn away from your own flesh and blood?"* (Isaiah 58:7).

Here are a few simple ideas to help the homeless:

- Volunteer with Habitat for Humanity; www.habitat.org
- Keep granola bars, food gift cards, dollar bills, etc. in your car;
- Inquire which item they need the most and purchase it (within reason). Baby formula? A sandwich? Inexpensive shoes?

Following through on these ideas may be challenging, yet God puts homeless people in our path to teach us compassion. Let's step outside of our comfort zones and show we are Christians by our love!

> *"Truly I tell you, whatever you did for one of the least of these brothers and sisters of mine, you did for me"* (Matthew 25:40).

Relational Tip #5
DON'T WASTE YOUR TIME WAITING

Life involves a lot of waiting. We wait at the airport, doctor's office, sporting events, etc. It's frustrating. And it just seems like wasted time.

The next time you find yourself waiting, ask God to give you an opportunity to witness. Pay attention to your surroundings. Make yourself available by silencing your phone and putting it away. Greet people with eye contact and a friendly hello. Perhaps you will notice another person who is not glued to their phone. Say hello. This could be a door God is opening. Trust the Holy Spirit to give you the words and to direct the conversation.

Time spent waiting is also well-invested by reading the Bible or memorizing Scripture. If you have your index cards from Personal Growth Tip #4 (Memorize and Meditate on God's Word), someone may even notice you and make a comment. And then the floor is yours.

Invitation Tips

#1 Step Outside Your "Holy Huddle"
#2 Carry Your Church's Business Cards
#3 Invite with Intent and They Will Come
#4 Bring a Friend to BSF
#5 Host an In-home Bible Study
#6 Invest in Mentoring

Invitation Tip #1
STEP OUTSIDE YOUR HOLY HUDDLE

We all like to hang out with people who are like us. Christians are no exception. Of course it should be a priority to fellowship with believers; however, how can we be the "salt and the light" if we don't step outside our "holy huddles"? Include unchurched families in picnics, beach outings, camping trips, holiday celebrations, youth group, even Bible studies and mission trips!

Pray that God would lay a specific unsaved person on your heart with whom to forge a relationship. For example: someone with whom you've had a rift; that person who doesn't "quite fit in;" or someone you've been wanting to get to know better. Call them today, figure out a time to meet, and ink it on the calendar!

Invitation Tip #2
CARRY YOUR CHURCH'S BUSINESS CARDS

As you go about your daily routine you come into contact with many people: retail clerks, work associates, contractors, hair stylists, etc. It can be quite easy to ask them if they have a good church. (Do not ask if they go to church because that can make them feel guilty or put them on the defensive.) If they answer "no," tell them how great your church is and give them a business card with the service times. Briefly describe where your church is located and restate the service times. Stash a few cards in your wallet or purse for such opportunities.

Occasionally people will confide in you that they are lonely, searching for a spouse, just moved to the area, or are just plain looking for something to do. Your church's business cards will be an excellent way to point them in the right direction!

Invitation Tip #3
INVITE WITH INTENT AND THEY WILL COME

"Most people come to church because of a personal invitation. But 7 out of 10 unchurched people have never been invited to church in their whole lives. As many as 82% of people would come to church if we invited them"[i]

As with any discipline, we must be intentional to get results. Do not invite people to church just to check a box. Invest time and effort. Build relationships. Prioritize their need to hear the gospel over your schedule. This is how, as Christians, we show our love. Here are some guidelines:

Be intentional. Ask God to identify some people to invite to church. Make a list of names. Identify a date and venue within the next month and invite someone.

Take a back seat. Subordinate your own scheduling difficulties in order to prioritize the need for others to hear the gospel.

Get excited! We love to recommend restaurants and movies—do the same for your church! Extol the praises of what a relationship with Christ has done for you!

Do not prejudge. Allow the Holy Spirit to guide your invitation process regardless of the others' faith (or lack thereof). God desires that none should perish. You will be surprised who will accept.

Drive them there. "80% of first-time visitors to church were driven."[10]

Combine your invitation with food. Invite your guest to share a meal afterwards, whether at your home or a restaurant. This demonstrates you are interested in a relationship more than just "pushing your faith."

Call in advance. Phone calls convey more personal interest and effort than a text or an email. Let your guest know how excited you are that they are joining you and clarify any logistics.

Confirm the day before. It is always good practice to confirm any appointment. Extend a personal call the day before church. A call shows the most personal investment, and it is harder to cancel with a live person then via email or text. If they cancel but tell you they still really want to come, get a date on the calendar immediately.

Introduce. If you see friends before or after service, be sure to introduce them to your guest. A friendly atmosphere encourages people to return. They may even run into some of their own friends.

Clarify. Ask if they learned anything new or need some clarification on what they heard. But don't beat them over the head!

Invite them back. If they want to return, assist them to get plugged into church with Bible studies, kids' programs, and service opportunities. If they seem apprehensive, do not be pushy. Let them know how happy you are that they came to church with you.

Continue the relationship. Demonstrate "that we are Christians by our love" by touching base with them every so often and including them in social activities.

INVITE TO A SPECIAL EVENT

Churches host a myriad of programs relevant to the public at large. This type of event could be a better entrée for some people than a church service. Examples of these programs include: Concerts, Financial Seminars (Dave Ramsey classes are phenomenal!), Parenting and Marriage Workshops, Vacation Bible School, Mothers of PreSchoolers (MOPS), Grief Sessions, etc.

Many people accept invitations to Easter and/or Christmas services even if they don't attend church the rest of the year.

There are also huge evangelical events across America, such as The Harvest Crusade and Promise Keepers. The stadiums are packed and it's amazing to feel the power of the Holy Spirit as hundreds, if not thousands, claim Christ as their Lord and Savior. Invite as many people as you can fit in your car and go!

Invitation Tip #4
BRING A FRIEND TO BSF

I cannot recommend Bible Study Fellowship (BSF) enough! BSF is available to men, women, and young adults and offers both morning and evening classes. Anyone can attend—whether you are a "Bible scholar" or have never opened God's Word. Currently there are over 1000 classes in 39 countries.

The goal of BSF is for each member to delve into God's Word and to grow in a vibrant relationship with Jesus Christ. Their approach to studying the Bible enables you to retain and share God's Word. The curriculum rotates through nine studies, some of which include: Genesis, The Life of Moses, The Gospel of John, and Revelation.

One unique aspect of Bible Study Fellowship is that each class around the world studies the same lesson at the same time. The classes run from September through May; however, you can join at any time during the year. BSF has a phenomenal program for preschoolers. It is not simply childcare--even the babies are taught the Word of God. BSF is free (even for the little ones).

Bible Study Fellowship will help hone your discipline to study the Bible. Your personal relationship with God can also grow tremendously as you learn to listen to what He is saying to you personally when you interact with His Word to answer the questions. Visit the BSF website today to register. Search by zip code to find the class nearest you. And don't forget to bring a friend!

<u>www.bsfinternational.org</u>

Invitation Tip #5
HOST AN IN-HOME STUDY

Hosting a Bible Study in your home doesn't mean you have to be the leader. And what a great strategy to get yourself there on time! Many churches seek homes for Bible Studies. Offer yours. Apartments, condos, and townhomes work, too. Cozy is nice.

When you host a Bible Study, you are utilizing the home that God has given you to "make disciples." Many people are wary of "stepping foot" into a church, so opening your home allows them the opportunity to learn God's Word.

My husband and I have some friends who initiated a Bible Study in their home. We meet Sunday evenings, socialize, and then watch a short video with a workbook (i.e. those by Rick Warren, Andy Stanley, etc.) and discuss our answers. Each session lasts five to eight weeks.

My husband and I enjoy the low-key atmosphere. Members are transparent and we are reminded that others face the same struggles we do. We learn how to maneuver life in God's will vs. what culture dictates. If there are unbelievers in the group, they recognize there is another way to navigate life. Praise God! Attendance is growing!

"They broke bread in their homes and ate together with glad and sincere hearts, praising God and enjoying the favor of all the people. And the Lord added to their number daily those who were being saved" (Acts 2:46-47).

The study is now rotating among the members to new homes with new leaders. This couple, obedient to God's calling to begin a Bible study in their home, are "making disciples" and equipping others to grow in their faith.

"...Solid food is for the mature, who by constant use have trained themselves to distinguish good from evil" (Hebrews 5:12-14).

Invitation Tip #6
INVEST IN MENTORING

Do you have a few hours to invest in the spiritual growth of another Christian? Changed lives attract others as they see the Spirit of God at work.

Mentor a New Christian

This does not have to take much time—maybe even just a few sessions. If you can answer basic questions about God, Jesus, sin, and salvation then you are qualified. The best method is to work as a pair to answer the new believer's questions. Once the new Christian can do this, they will be able to study the Bible on their own and in turn teach a new believer the same.

"As iron sharpens iron, so one person sharpens another" (Proverbs 27:17).

Mentor a Seasoned Christian

If you have expertise in different stages of life such as marriage, fatherhood, raising kids, etc., consider counseling other Christians who could benefit from your knowledge. For example, our marriage mentors taught us to pray before making decisions (both large and small). Seemingly obvious, this had never crossed our minds. You do not have to be perfect to be a mentor! On the contrary, allow others to learn from your mistakes.

Seek Out a Mentor

Seeking out a mentor is not a sign of weakness—it is a sign of strength to desire godly counsel. Mentors can provide trusted guidance in major life decisions. They can assist in establishing personal and spiritual goals, and help to monitor an appropriate balance of the two.

"Two are better than one because they have a good return for their labor: If either of them falls down, one can help the other up. But pity anyone who falls and has no one to help them up" (Ecclesiastes 4:9-10).

Service Tips

Service Tip #1
SPREAD SOME CHEER

Drive to the Doctor

A very real way to be the hands and feet of Jesus is to drive people to and from their doctor appointments. Quite frequently a patient will have a series of ongoing follow-up visits. Round up some friends to help or subdivide the appointments among your Bible Study group members.

Appointment times may not be convenient and wait times can be substantial, so it is very likely that this tip will not fit nicely into your busy schedule. Consider taking a vacation day. While this would be a sacrifice, consider what Jesus did for us.

"In the same way, let your light shine before others, that they may see your good deeds and glorify your Father in heaven" (Matthew 5:16).

Keep Company During Chemo

How about sitting with someone during chemotherapy? Usually there are multiple visits prescribed. Chemo sessions can last in excess of five hours! Imagine how wonderful it would be for the patient to have some company. Or for the caregiver to get a much-needed break.

Pick up the phone, select a date, and offer to drive the patient to the appointment or to meet at the facility. The time together is also an excellent way to gift a Bible or to share the gospel.

Because we are so uncomfortable when someone else has cancer (instead of us), we choose "not to bother them." Guess what? They want to hear from you! They need a distraction…some laughter in their lives. Let's step outside of ourselves and put the other person first!

"A generous person will prosper; whoever refreshes others will be refreshed" (Proverbs 11:25).

Service Tip #2
MINISTER WITH MEAL OPTIONS

Meals are a huge help to families when someone is ill, a baby has been born, etc. If you are unaware whether meals have been organized, just ask! If a list has been started, get on it. If not, coordinate the meals yourself. One good online tool is www.mealtrain.com

If you don't like to cook, order from an inexpensive local restaurant that you like and drive it over. Or, (especially if you are super busy or live too far to deliver a meal), email the recipient and let them know you really and truly want to provide them a meal. Remind them that "it is more blessed to give then to receive" (Acts 20:35). Ask them for the name of one of their favorite local restaurants (i.e. sandwiches, pasta, pizza, etc.) that has delivery. When your turn arrives and you place the order, call the recipient and remind them that tax and delivery has been paid.

Homemade dinners are wonderful, but at the end of the day it really is the thought that counts. What the recipient will remember is that you cared enough go out of your way to help.

While meals are a huge blessing, it can be exhausting for the recipients to talk to everyone who delivers a meal. Consider placing a table out front for the meals to be delivered with a note of thanks (perhaps framed). Folks who are in a hurry appreciate this too. Use disposable containers to further reduce the recipient's hassle of washing and returning dishes.

"Do to others as you would have them do to you" (Luke 6:31).

Service Tip #3
CHOOSE A NEW VACATION DESTINATION

When we think "vacation," images of relaxing on a chaise lounge, swimming in a resort pool, or even just some extra sleep come to mind. How about changing it up next year and trying out an action adventure? Go on a mission trip!

Mission trips aren't just for youth. It's eye-opening to check out some of the short-term opportunities that exist for people of all ages, including families, right here in the USA. Destinations include diverse locations such as Appalachia and New York City.

Consider these amazing benefits of mission trips:[11]

1.   Draw participants together and toward Jesus;
2.   Broaden perspectives;
3.   Challenge comfort zones;
4.   Empower; and
5.   Create "sacred space"—more than a mere "mountain top high"—a time and a place when God works in and through your life.

Mission trips can last for a day, or from a few days to a few months. If you would like to spend at least a few nights, search "short term mission trips in the United States" and let the adventure begin!

Single day opportunities include visiting orphanages, food banks, and shelters. Contact your church and register to attend one of the outings they have scheduled with partner organizations.

Service Tip #4
USE YOUR GOD-GIVEN GIFTS

Do I have a God-given gift? Yes! God has given each person gifts--unique skills and talents. God wants us to use these gifts to serve the church (the body of Christ), and to reach out to the unsaved. Even if you don't serve in the limelight, your talent is equally important to those who do.

"Even so the body is not made up of one part but of many...If the whole body were an eye, where would the sense of hearing be? If the whole body were an ear, where would the sense of smell be?" (1 Corinthians 12:14, 17).

What is my God-given gift? If you are unsure as to your God-given gift, ask the Christians with whom you associate. They can tell you because they know how you bless them!

Think about what you really enjoy doing: what you are good at? Perhaps it doesn't seem like a talent. If you can use it to bless others, it is. If certain social injustices boil your blood, God has given you both the desire and skills to serve in this capacity in the name of Jesus.

How can I use my God-given gifts? Connect and build relationships with unbelievers who share the same interests. Serve both in and outside the church. Here are a few ideas:

- **Computer science**: teach classes at the church to help the older generation "keep up" with technology;
- **Automotive**: tune up church vehicles; organize a group of high school youth and work at restoring a car;
- **Beauty**: gift women in a shelter with a Spa Day; conduct an event for youth on personal grooming tips and career skills.

"Each of you should use whatever gift you have received to serve others, as faithful stewards of God's grace in its various forms." (1 Peter 4:10).

Service Tip #5
TRAIN THEM UP

Jesus said, 'Let the little children come to me, and do not hinder them, for the kingdom of heaven belongs to such as these'" (Matthew 19:14).

Children's Ministry

God wants everyone to serve their church body—and Children's Ministry always needs help! Almost anyone can serve and needs exist throughout the week. A few positions include: holding babies, romping with toddlers, and teaching, assisting, or substituting for Preschool-5th grade. Other jobs include prepping class materials, confirming the volunteer schedule, and cleaning toys.

> *"Train up a child in the way he should go, and when he is old he will not depart from it" (Proverbs 22:6).*

Youth Group

Working with teenagers may seem daunting; however, stepping outside of your comfort zone will grow and bless you. Our youth not only need Christian role models, more increasingly they simply need someone who will show up regularly and take an interest in them. Bring the neighborhood youth, too. Many parents like their kids going to church even if they don't attend themselves.

Middle school and high school ministry opportunities exist year round. Volunteer at the snack shack, drive to activities, lead a study, or open your home for a special event. Strong male role models are especially crucial for our young men.

When my oldest began attending youth group, I was literally afraid to step foot inside their bungalow. I had no idea what to make of that age group. But when God prodded me to volunteer, I learned that youth are just trying to find their place in the world like the rest of us. In an ever-darkening world, the Lord used me to share kindness, wisdom, and hope in Christ that some students may not have otherwise heard. God can use you in that way, too.

Seasonal Tips

#1 Exercise This Constitutional Right

#2 Share Some Summer Fun

#3 Celebrate Halloween on the Driveway

#4 Champion "Operation Christmas Child"

Seasonal Tip #1
EXERCISE THIS CONSTITUTIONAL RIGHT

Are you happy about the fact that many of our Constitutional rights are becoming obsolete? Especially those of Christians? Registering to vote is the first step. A number of years ago I tried to distribute some political information at church and was stunned at how many Christians told me they were not registered to vote or that they knew nothing about the candidates!

Our right to vote was paid for by the blood of patriots, and our men and women in uniform still sacrifice their lives today for our freedom. Let's not lose the right to vote through apathy or disuse. Access the following website to register to vote or to renew your voter registration. www.usa.gov/register-to-vote

Some say, "Politicians just do whatever they want so my vote doesn't even count;" or, "Jesus is coming soon and this world is ending so what's the point?" Yet consider patients whose doctors have given them a bleak diagnosis. Will most of them just roll over? No! The majority will work hard to reverse their condition, or at least go out fighting and maintain the best quality of life possible until the end. So should Christians!

When voting season comes around, as in all activities, seek God's will. Toss the barrage of postcard propaganda. Meet and pray with other Christians to unravel the key candidates and legislation. Choose principles of right in place of selfish decisions. Refrain from voting blindly or out of a sense of party loyalty. Select the candidates and legislation most in line with Biblical principles.

Lastly, do not lessen you love for Christian brothers and sisters whose voting differs from yours. No one is infallible.

> *"I urge, then, first of all, that petitions, prayers, intercession and thanksgiving be made for all people— for kings and all those in authority, that we may live peaceful and quiet lives in all godliness and holiness" (1 Timothy 2:1-2).*

Seasonal Tip #2
SHARE SOME SUMMER FUN

All hands on deck! Summer is here and that means that soon it will be time for Vacation Bible School (VBS)! This is a HUGE community outreach program. Rosters book up fast—Christian and unchurched parents alike love their kids to attend VBS. So whether you volunteer, invite, or do both, you are "making disciples." The kids have such a blast that their parents come to church to check out what all the excitement is about!

It takes an unbelievable amount of effort (and expense) to pull off a successful VBS. Today's Vacation Bible School programs are not those of yesteryear! Now there are water slides, petting zoos, snow cones, dance troupes, and zip lines. One of the reasons God has given such an abundance of talents to His people is because every single one of them is necessary to prepare and execute Vacation Bible School!

Volunteers are needed for both advance planning and "week of" activities. Many churches offer both day and evening sessions. So no excuses---even if you have only three hours one day or night, come serve and share some summer fun at Vacation Bible School.

Seasonal Tip #3
CELEBRATE HALLOWEEN ON THE DRIVEWAY

Christians are called to be relational and to be the "salt and the light." Halloween is the only day of the year that neighbors you don't even know (and in a good mood), will walk right up to your doorstep. Instead of shutting off your lights or scurrying to a Harvest party (do this any night except Halloween), use the holiday for some fun evangelism!

Congregate with some other families (unsaved friends, too!) at a home that gets a lot of trick-or-treaters. Set up some tables and chairs in the driveway, and provide coffee for the parents, water bottles, and really good candy. Of course your church's business cards or gospel tracts too! (If packaged in a bag with the candy the information will have a better chance of getting home.)

While kids love to trick or treat and amass as much candy as possible, adults love the "treat" that the hot coffee and brief break provides. Spend a little time just chatting and getting to know them. Mention you attend a really great church, one great thing it's done for you, and give them a business card. That's probably enough unless they ask you a follow up question. You will be demonstrating that you are a Christian by your love.

Seasonal Tip #4
CHAMPION OPERATION CHRISTMAS CHILD

Have you ever packed a shoebox with toys and supplies for a child at Christmas? There is a good chance you were involved in the program called Operation Christmas Child.

Sponsored by Samaritans Purse, Operation Christmas Child provides over ten million shoeboxes (packed by people like you and me) to youth around the globe. Most of these kids live in war-torn and impoverished communities. Imagine the indescribable joy a child experiences when they receive their very own shoebox.

Not only are the shoeboxes provided in the name of Jesus Christ, a discipleship program is offered to most of the children. So when you participate in Operation Christmas Child, you are truly "making disciples of all nations."

Most people you tell about Operation Christmas Child will want to pack a shoebox. This enables everyone, Christian or otherwise, to experience the joy of giving at Christmas.

You can champion this cause by making it easier for others to participate. Distribute flyers and shoeboxes to people who want to contribute. Simplify the process by explaining the gender/age tag, where to shop, and recommended contents. Gather the shoeboxes and deliver them to the collection site.

Make it extra fun by coordinating and/or hosting packing parties with your work, school, sports team, or youth organization. Play a video clip at the event so participants can witness the joy their effort will bring to these youth.

> *"And if anyone gives even a cup of cold water to one of these little ones who is my disciple, truly I tell you, that person will certainly not lose their reward" (Matthew 10:42).*

Appendix A

Small Group Use of *Everyday Evangelism*

The pivotal component for success and growth through Everyday Evangelism is prayer and public group sharing of experiences relating to use of these tips. As members step out of their comfort zones, other group members will witness this and do the same.

Recommended timeframe: Six weeks is optimal.

Study guide: None. There is a weekly challenge to" choose and use" a tip.

Suggested weekly format:
1. Share the previous week's evangelism activities.
2. Read and discuss one, two, or three tip categories (and embedded scripture).
3. Weekly challenge: Each member chooses a tip they plan to use and shares it with the group.

Possible chapter flow:
In the initial meeting, prior to reviewing the tips, allow approximately ¼ of the time for the group to discuss previous experiences regarding evangelism. Brainstorm feelings about evangelism on a poster and save it for the last session.
Week 1: Biblical Reassurance Tips, Super Simple Tips
Week 2: Personal Growth Tips, Often-Forgotten Tips
Week 3: Gift Tips, Financial Tips
Week 4: Critical Conversation Tips—*Allot most of the time in this category to practicing the "Gospel Share" and "30-Second Testimony" Tips. Partner up and ask volunteers to model to group.*
Week 5: Relational Tips, Invitation Tips
Week 6: Service Tips, Seasonal Tips—*In conclusion, brainstorm the group's current feelings toward evangelism and compare it to the poster from the first week. Recap challenges and successes and share future goals.*

Appendix B

Congregational Use of *Everyday Evangelism*

The pivotal component for success and growth through Everyday Evangelism is prayer and public group sharing of experiences relating to use of these tips.

1. **Think Big.** Use this book as the basis for an evangelism campaign—provide an opportunity for your church to rally behind a common goal.
2. **Set Goals.** Involve all church staff and key members. Set achievable and measureable goals that align with the specific tips. Set start and end dates (3-6 months).
3. **Build Anticipation.** Use signage, the church website, stickers, "Coming Soon" references, etc. Invent a name for your campaign, i.e. "Action Figures for Christ," "Evangelism Every Day," or "Let Us Show We Are Christians by Our Love."
4. **Design the Procedure.** Ideas: 1) The congregation reads a chapter weekly and the sermons correlate with the material. 2) Use this book in your church-wide Bible studies. 3) Form action teams for each tip category.
5. **Share weekly as a congregation via open-mic.** *This is crucial to the success of your campaign. What this will achieve:*
    *   Positive peer pressure (members will witness what their peers can do and want to do the same);
    *   The realization that God calls all Christians to evangelize (not just the pastoral staff);
    *   A platform for your members to step out of their comfort zones and become lifestyle evangelists; and
    *   A more vibrant, energetic, unified church community.

Bibliography

1   Rainier, Dr. Thom. *The Unchurched Next Door*. Grand Rapids, Michigan: Zondervan, 2008. 272. Print.

2   "America's Changing Religious Landscape." *Pew Research Centers Religion Public Life Project RSS*. 11 May 2015. Web. 22 Sept. 2015

3   Scholtes, Peter R. *They Will Know We Are Christians*. 1966. Web.

4   *Dictionary.com*. Web. 22 Sept. 2015. "compassion" definition 1.

5   Maurer, Rich. "Not Proselytize." *YouTube*. 13 Nov. 2009. Web. 28 Jan. 2016.

6   Ortlund, Dane. "Bible Q&A - Why Read the Bible Every Day?" *Crossway Blog*. 19 Aug. 2014. Web. 29 Dec. 2015.

7   *King James Version*. Bible Gateway. Web. 4 Jan. 4, 2016.

8   "Social Networking Use." *Pew Research Center RSS*. 29 Nov. 2012. Web. 24 Aug. 2015.

9   Abraham, Felicia. "10 Ways to Evangelize on Facebook." *Charisma Magazine*. 5 Dec. 2012. Web. 24 Aug. 2015.

10 *The Urban Alternative*. Senior Pastor Tony Evans. KWAVE, San Clemente. Radio.

11 Townsend, Sam. "5 Reasons Every Teenager Should Go On a Mission Trip." *Youthworks*. 11 Feb. 2014. Web. 24 Aug. 2015.